Endangered Lizards
Colouring Book

In Support of the
Sri Lanka Wildlife Conservation Society
http://www.slwcs.org/

Written and illustrated by
Jay Manchand

An Earth Apps Book
My Fat Fox Ltd
MMXIV

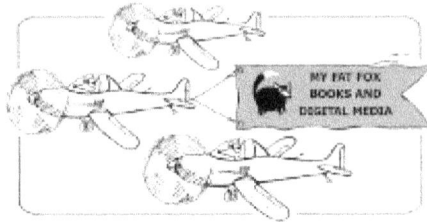

My Fat Fox Ltd
86 Gladys Dimson House
London E7 9DF
United Kingdom
www.myfatfox.co.uk

Endangered Lizards Colouring Book
© 2014 Jay Manchand

www.environment.myfatfox.co.uk/jay_manchand.html

Cover design
© 2014 Jay Manchand and Hartmut Jager

http://hartmut–jager.artistwebsites.com/

ISBN 978-1-905747-37-5

For Chris

"The good life is one inspired by love
and guided by knowledge"

~BERTRAND RUSSELL

About the author

For as long as he can remember, Jay Manchand has had a passion for reptiles and amphibians; his mother would often find him sitting in her pond 'playing' with frogs. Also a keen artist, he has learned to transfer that passion onto paper and canvas. Jay hopes to use his acute attention to detail to encourage others to see the astonishing beauty and intrigue of these underdogs of the animal kingdom.

TABLE OF CONTENTS

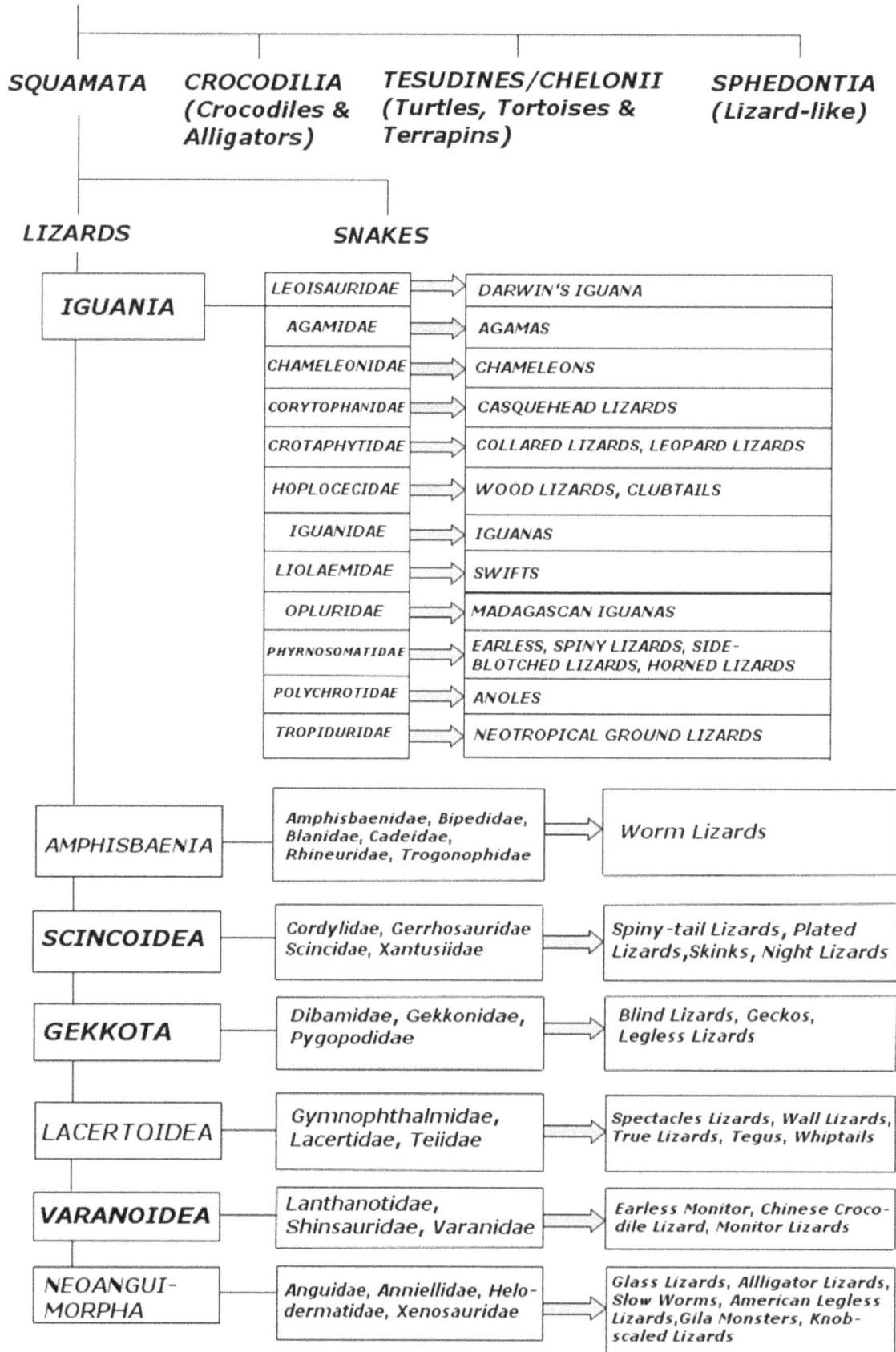

Taxonomic Table

REPTILIA

SQUAMATA	CROCODILIA (Crocodiles & Alligators)	TESUDINES/CHELONII (Turtles, Tortoises & Terrapins)	SPHEDONTIA (Lizard-like)

LIZARDS   **SNAKES**

IGUANIA

Family	Common Name
LEOISAURIDAE	DARWIN'S IGUANA
AGAMIDAE	AGAMAS
CHAMELEONIDAE	CHAMELEONS
CORYTOPHANIDAE	CASQUEHEAD LIZARDS
CROTAPHYTIDAE	COLLARED LIZARDS, LEOPARD LIZARDS
HOPLOCECIDAE	WOOD LIZARDS, CLUBTAILS
IGUANIDAE	IGUANAS
LIOLAEMIDAE	SWIFTS
OPLURIDAE	MADAGASCAN IGUANAS
PHYRNOSOMATIDAE	EARLESS, SPINY LIZARDS, SIDE-BLOTCHED LIZARDS, HORNED LIZARDS
POLYCHROTIDAE	ANOLES
TROPIDURIDAE	NEOTROPICAL GROUND LIZARDS

AMPHISBAENIA

Families	Common Name
Amphisbaenidae, Bipedidae, Blanidae, Cadeidae, Rhineuridae, Trogonophidae	Worm Lizards

SCINCOIDEA

Families	Common Name
Cordylidae, Gerrhosauridae Scincidae, Xantusiidae	Spiny-tail Lizards, Plated Lizards, Skinks, Night Lizards

GEKKOTA

Families	Common Name
Dibamidae, Gekkonidae, Pygopodidae	Blind Lizards, Geckos, Legless Lizards

LACERTOIDEA

Families	Common Name
Gymnophthalmidae, Lacertidae, Teiidae	Spectacles Lizards, Wall Lizards, True Lizards, Tegus, Whiptails

VARANOIDEA

Families	Common Name
Lanthanotidae, Shinsauridae, Varanidae	Earless Monitor, Chinese Crocodile Lizard, Monitor Lizards

NEOANGUI-MORPHA

Families	Common Name
Anguidae, Anniellidae, Helodermatidae, Xenosauridae	Glass Lizards, Alligator Lizards, Slow Worms, American Legless Lizards, Gila Monsters, Knob-scaled Lizards

Lizard Families

Geckos

With around 1,500 known species in the world, Geckos were originally defined by their ability to communicate with each other through a variety of chirps and barks – each one unique depending on the species. Most Geckos do not have eyelids; instead they have a thin membrane to protect the eye. Geckos will often lick their own eyes to keep them moist and clean. Geckos are great climbers and are easily able to climb smooth surfaces such as glass. The majority of these small lizards are smooth skinned and able to 'drop' their tails as a defence mechanism.

Iguanas

Possibly one of the most recognised species of lizards, and particularly common in the Reptile pet hobby, is the Iguana, especially the Green Iguana. The typical Iguana has a large, stocky build with a long powerful tail which is used as a whip when under threat. With a row of spiny scales running from its neck to back and a range of coloured scales within its species, these lizards are excellent at camouflage and evading predators. Iguanas have what is called a 'third eye' or a 'Parietal eye'. It appears as a lighter scale on the top of their head. The Parietal eye is used for thermoregulation – making the lizard aware if its body is either too hot or too cold - and it is sensitive to light and dark and almost works as a body clock. Iguanas communicate through gestures, such as head bobbing.

Monitor Lizards

A very intelligent species of lizards, Monitor lizards range in size from the Short-tailed Monitor at just 20cm to the 9ft kings of the reptile world, the Komodo Dragons. In the wild, Monitor lizards will stand on their hind legs and 'monitor' their surroundings for predators and prey alike, hence their name. These agile lizards are great climbers and can live in many different environments; some are adept swimmers and spend much of their time in water. Most Monitor lizards are carnivorous, feeding on small mammals, eggs and carrion but there are newly discovered species of frugivorous (fruit eating) Monitor Lizards such as the Golden Spotted Monitor. Monitor lizards have a long forked tongue which is extremely sensitive and is used in the same way a Snake does, to pick up different scents.

Anoles

Generally a small lizard, there are over 370 different species of Anoles. Green & Brown Anoles are the most recognised in America and are often referred to as American Chameleons due to their ability to change colour depending on their mood and surroundings. Male Anoles are very territorial and will bob their heads as a warning to other males. They also conceal brightly coloured dewlaps, which are flaps of skin and cartilage on their throat. They can spread these out to impress females and to warn off predators and other males. When an Anole 'drops' its tail as a defence mechanism, the tail will continue to move vigorously to draw away the attention of its attacker, enabling the Anole to make a hasty escape.

Chameleons

Perhaps the most intriguing of lizard species, there are around 160 known Chameleon species. Chameleons are able to change colour to reflect their mood, to help camouflage themselves in their surroundings, and males change bright colours to impress females. Chameleons are distinguished by their eyes which move independently, an efficient way of hunting and staying alert from predators. They are also distinguished by their pincer-like feet which are split into groups of 2 digits facing one way and 3 digits facing another, giving the Chameleon astonishing grip and aiding it in climbing. Possibly the most interesting characteristic of these lizards is their method of eating. They have an unusually long extendible tongue that shoots out at an incredible speed, sticking to its prey and drawing the insect back into its mouth.

LIZARD SPECIES

The term 'endangered' is the conservation status of a species which indicates its population in relation to our saying goodbye to it.

This term covers all of the middle 3 categories below because their population numbers are in flux.

The final category isn't an IUCN, International Union for Conservation of Nature, endangered category but lately it has been used by conservation groups and it gives us hope.

Extinct
Extinct in the Wild

Critically Endangered
Endangered
Vulnerable

Near Threatened
Least Concerned

Recovered/ Comebacks

The drawings in the Earth Apps Collection can be coloured by coloured pencils, crayons, felt tips, and watercolours or with anything you'd like to use, though we advise against using marker pens as they may bleed through to the page below.

For more information about the Earth Apps collection please go to www.environment.myfatfox.co.uk.

Arboreal Alligator Lizard
(Abronia Graminea)

The Arboreal Alligator Lizard's habitat is under threat of land clearing for agricultural purposes. This lizard has a 'prehensile' tail, which means its tail has the ability to grasp branches, as if having an extra limb, making this lizard an expert climber. Also, the Arboreal Alligator Lizard gives birth to live young, which is very uncommon since the majority of lizards and other Reptiles lay eggs.

Colours:

Dark green with a yellow chin and yellow eyes.

How to help the Arboreal Alligator Lizard

Cocha Cashu Biological Station

http://cochacashu.sandiegozooglobal.org/home/cocha-cashu-in-a-nutshell/
(**shortened to:** http://tinyurl.com/cosha-cashu)

Manu National Park

http://www.visitmanu.com/en/

http://newscenter.berkeley.edu/2014/02/18/manu-national-park-in-peru-sets-new-biodiversity-record/

(**shortened to:** http://tinyurl.com/peru-manu)

http://www.manuwildlifecenter.com/manu-wildlife-center-facts.htm
(**shortened to:** http://tinyurl.com/manu-facts)

Boyd's Forest Dragon
(Hypsilurus Boydii)

Boyd's Forest Dragons spend much of their time perched on tree trunks waiting to ambush prey. They use their excellent camouflage to escape predators such as birds. Males of this species are very territorial, guarding hundreds of meters of the forest, fending off any male intruders. The Boyd's Forest Dragon lives in the wet tropics of Queensland. Global warming is likely to affect the climate of this already decreasing lizard.

Colours:

Males are bright green. Females are dark green or black with bright orange and yellow patterns.

How to help the Boyd's Forest Dragon

Rainforest Rescue

http://www.rainforest-rescue.org/

Donate: http://www.rainforest-rescue.org/donate

Australian Wildlife Conservancy

http://www.australianwildlife.org/

Donate: https://support.australianwildlife.org/

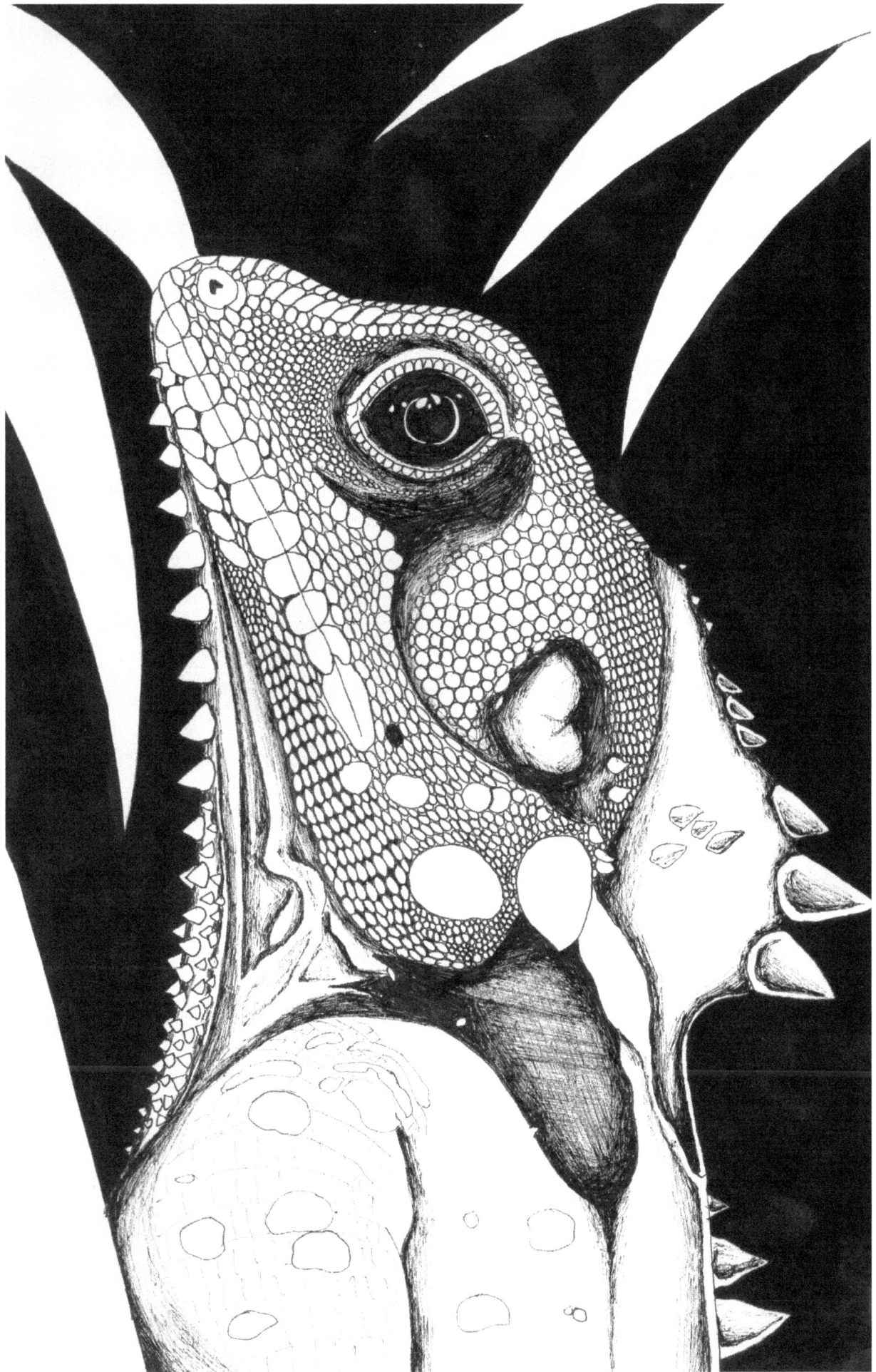

Cayman Blue Iguana
(Cyclura Lewisi)

The most endangered iguana on Earth, habitat destruction and feral pets such as cats & dogs have led to the near extinction of these beautiful creatures. Living solitary lives, males and females come together only during mating season, where the males change colour from a dull blue/grey to a bright blue to impress the females. There are breeding programmes in place in an attempt to prevent the loss of the Blue Iguana. Their population has risen to around 750 in the wild, thanks to these efforts.

Colours:

Bright blue with some grey scales around mouth and chin, with bright red eyes.

How to help the Cayman Blue Iguana

Smithsonian National Zoological Park

http://nationalzoo.si.edu/Animals/ReptilesAmphibians/Exhibit/Topics/iguana_conservation.cfm
(**shortened to:** http://tinyurl.com/smith-igua)

Donate:
https://org.salsalabs.com/o/1483/t/8832/p/salsa/donation/common/public/?donate_page_KEY=4607
(**shortened to:** http://tinyurl.com/igua-donate)

National Trust for the Cayman Islands

http://www.nationaltrust.org.ky/

Donate: http://www.nationaltrust.org.ky/index.php/donate

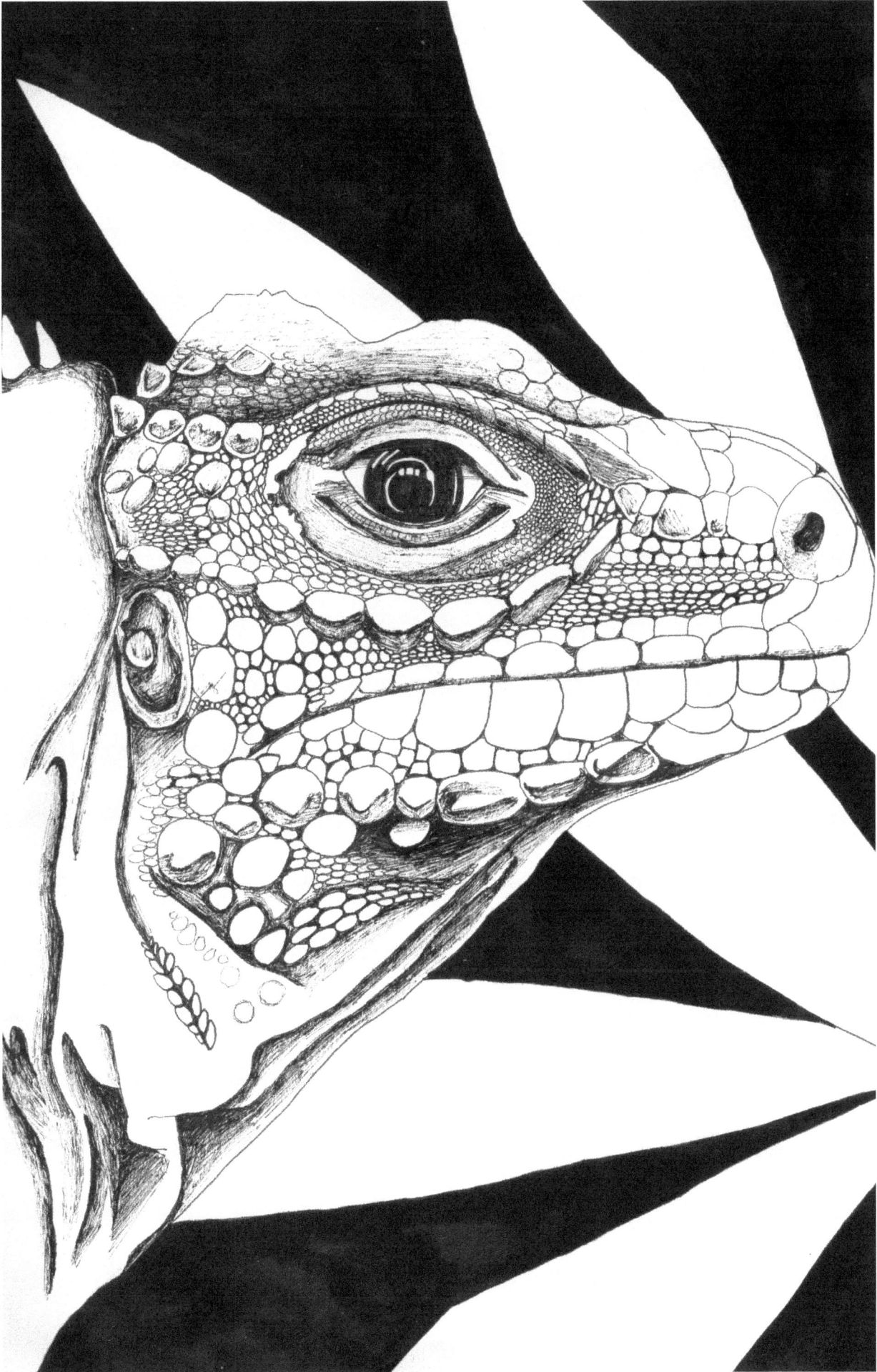

Galapagos Pink Iguana
(Conolophus Marthae)

The Galapagos Pink Iguana is considered a critically endangered species with as little as around 100 known adults. It is in fact so rare that even naturalist & explorer Charles Darwin missed discovering this species during his visit to the Galapagos in the 1800's and it wasn't until 2009 that the mysterious species was documented for the first time. Some of the Iguana's predators include the Galapagos Hawk, Black Rats & feral cats.

Colours:

Pink with grey and black patches of skin.

How to help the Galapagos Pink Iguana

Galapagos Conservation Trust

www.savegalapagos.org
Blog: www.galapagosblog.org

Donate: www.savegalapagos.org/getinvolved

Shop: http://www.savegalapagos.org/shop/

Page on the Galapagos Pink Iguana:

www.savegalapagos.org/news/2011/03/a-new-pink-iguana.shtml
(**shortened to:** http://tinyurl.com/pink-igua)

Galapagos Conservancy

http://www.galapagos.org/newsroom/gnp-news-pink-iguana-
monitoring/
(**shortened to:** http://tinyurl.com/pink-igua-news)

Donate: https://www.galapagos.org/connect-with-galapagos-
2/donate/
(**shortened to:** http://tinyurl.com/pink-igua-donate)

Hump Snout Lizard
(Lyriocephalus Scutatus)

Another lizard threatened by the illegal pet trade and habitat loss, the Hump Snout Lizard is a rare species from Sri Lanka. When competing for a female's attention, the male Hump Snout Lizard puffs out a bright coloured 'flap' of skin which it uses to entice the female and ward off its male rivals. This slow-moving lizard appears brown as a juvenile but develops much brighter colours as it reaches adulthood.

Colours:

Bright blue/turquoise, with a yellow underside and orange under the tail.

How to help the Hump Snout Lizard

Sri Lanka Wildlife Conservation Society

http://www.slwcs.org/

Donate: http://www.slwcs.org/donate.html

Sri Lanka Reptile - Wildreach

http://www.wildreach.com/reptile/Serpentes/

Rough Guide to Sri Lankas' National Parks, Reserves and Eco-tourism

http://www.roughguides.com/destinations/asia/sri-lanka/national-parks-reserves-eco-tourism/
(**shortened to:** http://tinyurl.com/rg-sri-lanka)

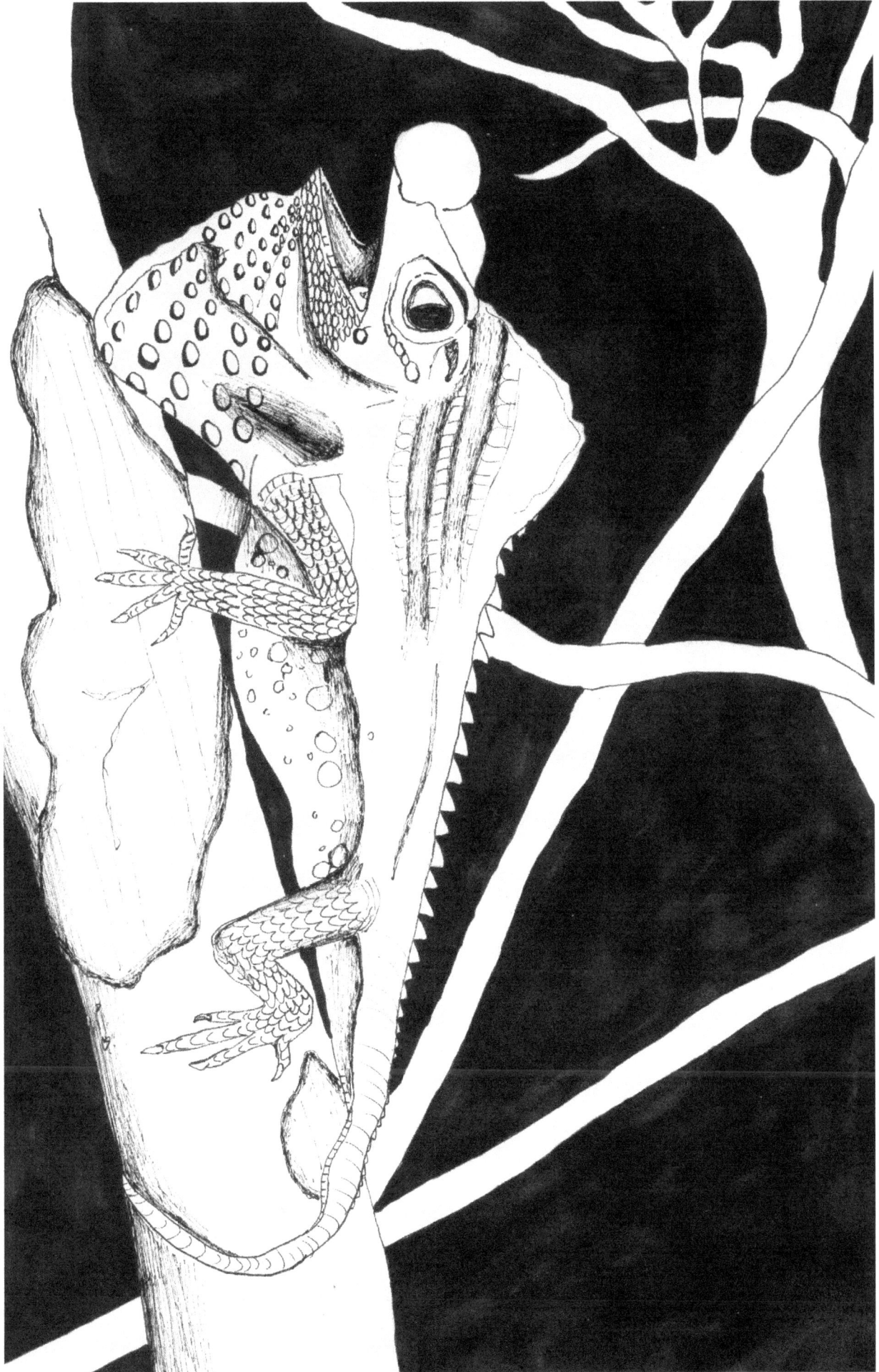

Komodo Dragon
(Varanus Komodoensis)

The largest and most powerful lizard on earth, the Komodo Dragon's mouth is filled with a poisonous bacteria and when hunting, the huge Monitor Lizard delivers a painful bite releasing a deadly concoction of venom and poison. Whilst the animal is weakened by the bite, the Komodo Dragon will stalk its prey, sometimes for days and often in small groups, until the animal is too weak to fight back or escape. Komodo Dragons are thought to be declining in the wild mainly due to poaching, habitat loss and volcanic activity.

Colours:

Brown with yellow around eyes.

How to help the Komodo Dragon

San Diego Zoo

http://animals.sandiegozoo.org/animals/komodo-dragon?qt-animals_page_content_tabs=3#qt-animals_page_content_tabs
(**shortened to:** http://tinyurl.com/sand-komodo)

Donate:
https://secure3.convio.net/sdzoo/site/Donation2?5000.donation=form1&df_id=5000
(**shortened to:** http://tinyurl.com/sand-donate)

Smithsonian National Zoo

http://nationalzoo.si.edu/animals/reptilesamphibians/facts/factsheets/komododragon.cfm
(**shortened to:** http://tinyurl.com/smith-komodo)

Donate:
https://org.salsalabs.com/o/1483/t/8832/p/salsa/donation/common/public/?donate_page_KEY=4607
(**shortened to:** http://tinyurl.com/smith-donate)

Labord's Chameleon
(Furcifer Labordi)

With the shortest lifespan ever recorded of a four-legged animal, Labord's Chameleons live for just 4-5 months after hatching, giving them only a little time to find a mate for reproducing. Found in Madagascar, the male of this species has an unusual hornlike protrusion from its head which it uses to fight other males when competing for a female. In most chameleons, the male has bright colours to attract females.

Colours:

Males are bright green. Females are dark green or black with bright orange and yellow patterns.

How to help the Labord's Chameleon

Madagasikara Voakajy

http://www.madagasikara-voakajy.org/

Donate: http://www.madagasikara-voakajy.org/index.php?option=com_content&view=article&id=5%3Asupport-us&catid=14%3Aabout-us&Itemid=3&lang=en-GB
(**shortened to:** http://tinyurl.com/madag-donate)

Conservation International Madagascar and Indian Ocean Islands

http://www.conservation.org/projects/Pages/madagascar-communities-profit-from-forest-conservation-ambositra-vondrozo-corridor.aspx
 (**shortened to:** http://tinyurl.com/cons-mada)

Donate: http://www.conservation.org/donate

Leaf-tailed Gecko
(Uroplatus Finivana)

Found in the forests of northern Madagascar, this nocturnal Leaf-tailed Gecko earns its name due to the large tail that expertly resembles a leaf. The Leaf-tailed Gecko uses this tail as a defence mechanism by confusing its predators; it also comes in handy when sneaking up on unsuspecting prey. Although not yet endangered, this Gecko's natural habitat in the National Park of Montagne D'ambre is under immediate future threats such as logging, deforestation & agricultural clearing.

Colours:

Mostly brown with yellow highlights.

How to help the Leaf-tailed Gecko

UNESCO World Heritage Centre

http://whc.unesco.org/en/list/1203

Donate: http://whc.unesco.org/en/donation

Sevalanka Foundation

http://www.sevalanka.org/Biodiversity_2013.html
(**shortened to:** http://tinyurl.com/lanka-bio)

Donate: http://www.sevalanka.org/donate.html
(**shortened to:** http://tinyurl.com/lanka-donate)

Philippine Sailfin Dragon
(Hydrosaurus Pustulatus)

Named after its sail-like fin along its tail, the Philippine Sailfin Dragon is an impressively large lizard and an adept swimmer with large flattened toes to help the lizard swim and run across the water's surface. It also has the ability to stay under water for up to 15 minutes when escaping from predators. Although successfully kept in captivity, the Sailfin Dragon is another victim of habitat loss and deforestation.

Colours:

Brown with a black head and blue scales and spikes.

How to help the Philippine Sailfin Dragon

Philippines Biodiversity Conservation Programme

www.tiertausch.de/Sailfin.htm

The Biodiversity Group

http://biodiversitygroup.org/topics/reptiles.html
(**shortened to:** http://tinyurl.com/biodiv-rept)

Pinocchio Anole
(Anolis Proboscis)

Thought to be already extinct, the Pinocchio Anole, also known as the Pinocchio Lizard, was recently rediscovered in the tropical cloud forests of Ecuador. Only spotted a few times in the past 15 years, these long-horned lizards can be found high up the forest canopy where they are extremely well camouflaged. The Pinocchio Anole moves especially slowly, most likely to avoid catching the attention of predators.

Colours:

Light green, with dark blue markings across the body. Some white patches on tail.

How to help the Pinocchio Anole

World Land Trust

http://www.worldlandtrust.org/projects/ecuador
(**shortened to:** http://tinyurl.com/wlt-ecua)

Buy an Acre

http://www.worldlandtrust.org/projects/buy-acre
(**shortened to:** http://tinyurl.com/ecua-buy-acre)

Nature and Culture International

http://natureandculture.org/countries/cloudforests

(**shortened to:** http://tinyurl.com/nci-cloud)

Donate: http://natureandculture.org/how-to-donate

(**shortened to:** http://tinyurl.com/nci-donate)

Tarzan's Chameleon
(Calumma Tarzan)

One of the one hundred most endangered species in the world, the Tarzan's Chameleon lives in a tiny forest near a small village in Madagascar called Tarzanville, hence the Chameleon's name. Another contribution to the name of this small Chameleon was from an evolutionary biologist who suggested that "Tarzan stands for jungle hero and fighting for protecting the forest". The Tarzan's Chameleon is considered more of a terrestrial (ground dwelling) lizard, living in wet forest plants up to 4 metres high.

Colours:

Green body, yellow stripes and a light brown casque (top of head).

How to help the Tarzan's Chameleon

World Wildlife Fund - Madagascar

https://www.worldwildlife.org/places/madagascar
(**shortened to:** http://tinyurl.com/wwf-mad)

Donate (and get 'thank you' apparel or Adopt a Species):

http://gifts.worldwildlife.org/gift-center/

Planet Madasgascar

http://www.planetmadagascar.com/

Donate: http://www.planetmadagascar.com/get-involved/
(**shortened to:** http://tinyurl.com/plan-mad-donate)

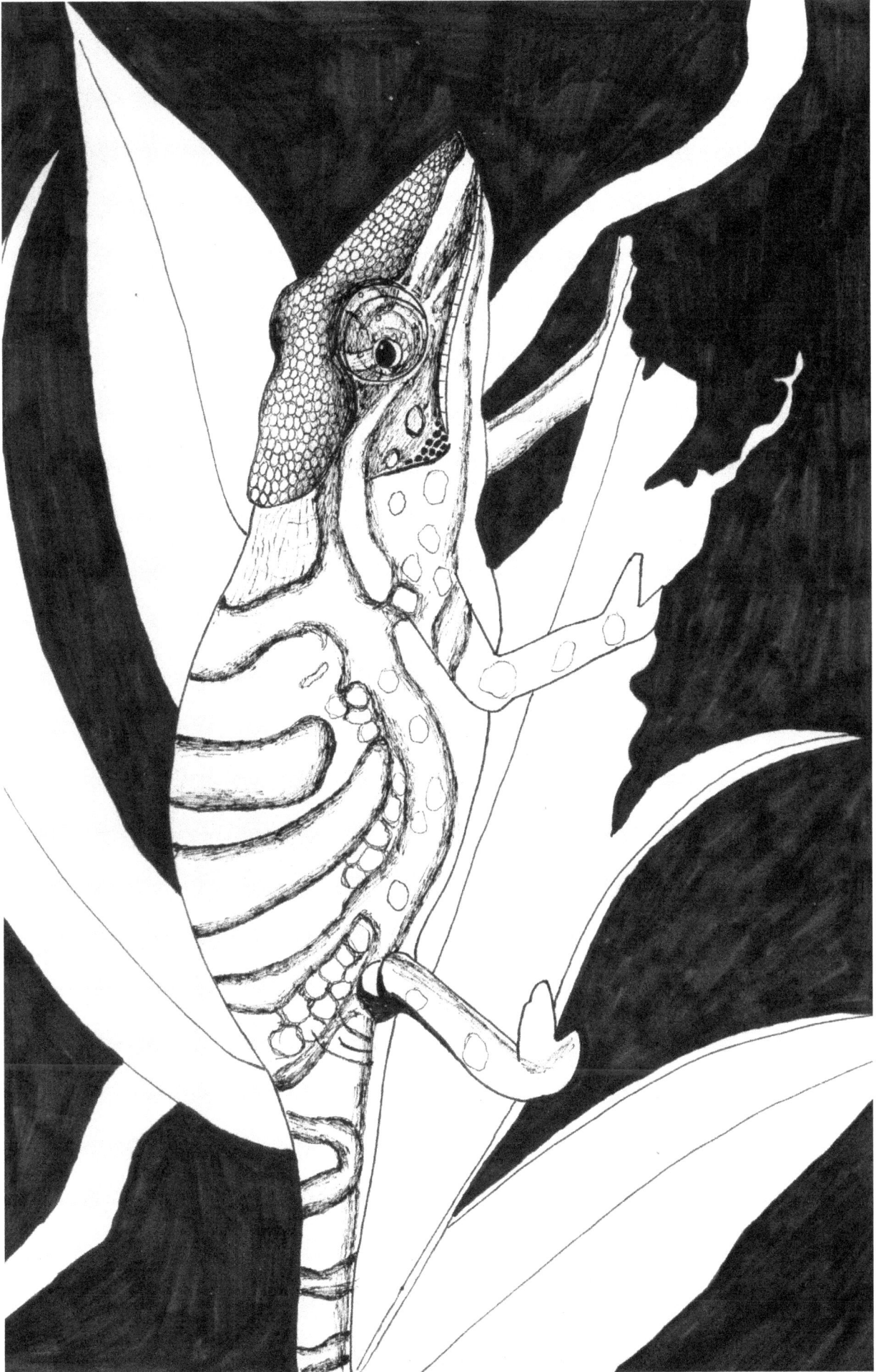

William's Dwarf Gecko
(Lygodactylus Williamsi)

Also known as the Turquoise Dwarf Gecko, the William's Dwarf Gecko is a small lizard, reaching 8cm as an adult. Its striking colours make it a sought-after animal in the pet trade, which has led to its unfortunate rapid decline in the wild due to illegal international pet trading. When captive bred, the William's Dwarf Gecko make hardy pets which are fascinating creatures to watch if a proper environment is maintained.

Colours:

Bright blue/turquoise, with a yellow underside and orange under the tail.

How to help the William's Dwarf Gecko

Tanzania Forest Conservation Group

http://www.tfcg.org/docs/about_us.htm

Wildlife Conservation Society

http://www.wcs.org/where-we-work/africa/tanzania.aspx
(**shortened to:** http://tinyurl.com/wcs-tanz)

Donate :

https://secure3.convio.net/wcs/site/SPageNavigator/Donation_main
.html
(**shortened to:** http://tinyurl.com/wcs-donate)

HOW TO HELP LIZARDS IN THE WILD

Endangered Species International

"From http://www.endangeredspeciesinternational.org/reptiles6.html

(**shortened to:** http://tinyurl.com/esi-rept)

what can you do to save reptiles?

- Don't buy products (particularly when you're abroad) made from reptile skins (e.g. handbags, boots made from snake or crocodile skin, jewellery made from tortoiseshell).

- Don't buy pets if you don't know where they are from – ongoing trade in reptile products has a huge effect on the numbers of valuable species in the wild. Even buying tropical species from legal sources increases demand and encourages illegal trading.

- Join reptile conservation groups and programmes such as Endangered Species International, and aid their efforts to conserve threatened species and habitats.

- Support legislation worldwide to administer and enforce wildlife conservation and trade laws to protect the most vulnerable species. This could include sending letters to authorities of causes championed by conservation organisations.

- Encourage preservation of nature, and the creation of parks and protected areas.

- Help in the fight to minimise global warming by reducing your own carbon footprint, and supporting decision-makers who are fighting climate change."

Center for Biological Diversity

Donate/Store:
https://org.salsalabs.com/o/2167/t/6268/shop/shop.jsp?storefront_KEY=258

(**shortened to:** http://tinyurl.com/cbd-storefront)

HOW TO HELP
ABANDONED PET LIZARDS

RSPCA - Reptile

http://www.rspcareptilerescue.co.uk/

Donate: https://mydonate.bt.com/fundraisers/keithwells1

Swindon Rescue Centre

http://www.swindonreptilerescue.com/about-us.html

Donate: http://www.swindonreptilerescue.com/donate.html

www.ingramcontent.com/pod-product-compliance
Lightning Source LLC
Chambersburg PA
CBHW081422270326
41931CB00015B/3373